THE MINING CAMPS

OF THE MOUTH

GEORGE KALAMARAS

THE MINING CAMPS
OF THE MOUTH

GEORGE KALAMARAS

NEW MICHIGAN PRESS

TUCSON, ARIZONA

NEW MICHIGAN PRESS

DEPT OF ENGLISH, P. O. BOX 210067

UNIVERSITY OF ARIZONA

TUCSON, AZ 85721-0067

<http://newmichiganpress.com/nmp>

Orders and queries to nmp@thediagram.com.

ISBN 978-1-934832-35-6. FIRST PRINTING.

Printed in the United States of America.

Design by Ander Monson.

Cover Photo: "Climax Mine Tailings Pond" (Climax
Mine, Leadville, Colorado), by Mark Ewing,
Foresight Aerial Photography (Denver, Colorado).

CONTENTS

HOUSE OF GREEN BUFFALO HIDES

3 Me. Mine. Moist. Exposed in the Medicine Bow

5 The Death of Nikola Tesla

7 House of Green Buffalo Hides. Slabs of Hump at Right, January 1882

11 A Theory of Taxidermy

13 Amnesia of the Hardboiled Detective Novel

16 Letter to Forrest from Laramie

18 Letter to Michelle from Victor

21 The Antelope Tree

22 Colorado Sheep Wars, 1894

THE WATER TRADE

27 The Water Trade

WORDS HELD BEFORE IN THE MOUTHS OF THE DEAD

39 The Mining Camps of the Mouth

42 Katya Whitcomb

44 Elegy for John Cipollina: Electric Guitar Gunslinger

47 History of a Drowned Door

49 Third Elegy

53 The Grave Witchers

58 Dream in Which Frank Waters Is My Mother

60 I'm Writing Gene a Letter

A PREFACE TO THE WEST

65   Preface to the Second Edition of the West

73   *Notes*
75   *Acknowledgments*

for John Bradley,
who read these poems, one at a time,
as they arrived on the loping rails
of our letters

Promise to whatever is promised
Love to whatever is loved
Ghosts to whatever is ghosts

—Jack Spicer

HOUSE OF GREEN BUFFALO HIDES

ME. MINE. MOIST. EXPOSED IN THE MEDICINE BOW

with a first line by Jack Spicer

Love to whatever is loved.

Open like granite
exposed in the Medicine Bow.

1. For a long time, I've lived as an owl on fire in my chest
2. Stars sink their thoroughly sunken into me

I am circling above you as if from below.

I am long and hard and always turning
into my lockjaw self.

The liana in the yard is homesick for the dahlia
drawing last month's rain up out of hard ground.

Open a granite rock out on the Rawhide Flats.
Like medicine. Like thick and slow and home.

I do not pour out of myself.
Go to your room now and meditate.

On fire. An owl is on fire in my chest.

1. Sincere and snow-blown quiet
2. Language that blurs and buries itself in the body like an osculant ox

Let a bird speak. Let me my talk and now (me, mine, moist).

Most of all I hold a damp wound in my bone.
Wind-drafts conjugating birds current
lines of a poem, fierce and full of mending.

Pouring. I do not pour out of my mouth.
Nor you, your left big toe.

The Western sky is somehow always east.
Colorado is both east and west of grief.

A piercingly blue sky.

                    I am aching for you wherever you go.

THE DEATH OF NIKOLA TESLA

When Nikola Tesla died, a little light went out from
his groin. Sparrows pulled apart from his dead belly
to reveal nomadic paths of bees, all alight with the
northern lights repeating themselves on journeys from
Namibia to Brazil. Telegrams poured in from the four
corners of grief: Buffalo Bill proclaimed from his grave
that this is what happens when you kill the cow before
the bull; César Vallejo copied *Tesla* over and again into
the skin of five notebooks, in the script of three different
hands; Admiral Peary and roustabout Cook said the
feud was finally over, that there never really was a North
Pole to dispute anyway; and Edison wept near his
recorder, nearly electrocuting himself on the magnetic
pull of the frayed cord. The good people of Colorado
Springs, where Tesla had lived, gathered in black on
a rare day of rain and feared the light might one day
even go out of their religion. The indigenous tribes of
Cheyenne Mountain journeyed to Pikes Peak to try to
capture afternoon lightning, though they knew the Peak
by names less certain of posterity. Nocturnal animals
shifted from *possums* to *opossums, stink-badgers* to
skunks, blaming rogue sparks of moonlight in the not-
yet-buried sun for their confused callings. *Tesla had died
as he had died*, the barn owl hooted all light long. *He will
live, now, also as he has died*. Nikolai and Pavlo and Yuri
left the saloon and wondered why lamps in their mining

hats had dimmed. Why their words were somehow
stuck in their throats, even after shots of whiskey and
a beer back. The poets spoke in the strange way poets
speak: Karl Marx proclaimed, *Death is the opiate of the
people*; John Bradley responded, *Rain pours through rain
even when it rains*; Joe Gastiger guarded the grave and
kept calling everyone *Darling* in the most adorable way;
and Vallejo—Vallejo said nothing, fingering, instead,
the outline of his skeleton through a suit coat that had
grown too large, a skeleton he had washed every day,
that somehow in Tesla's death glowed in Paris or Peru
with the auroras borealis of a life well-deathed.

HOUSE OF GREEN BUFFALO HIDES.
SLABS OF HUMP AT RIGHT, JANUARY 1882

based on a photograph by L. A. Huffman

"*The hunter usually shot the first buffalo through the lungs
so that it would bleed and totter for a little while before it
dropped. The others nearby would then become curious and
smell or hook the wounded animal, thus concentrating their
attention on the victim and not on the source of the danger.*"

—Mark H. Brown and W. R. Felton, *The Frontier Years*

1.

A sitting position with rest sticks
was preferred by most,
two to three hundred yards downwind
of what would die. *Make the kill
in as small an area as possible*, he had said,
as if discourse might serve to distance death itself.

2.

I'm writing a letter to a possum,
begging it to remain dark to the day.
Come out only at night, I plead. Emerge
through the pores of women
who wash the sheets of Denver and hang them
out on lines to moisten the not-yet-sunken moon.

3.

Judging from his notes, the photographer
seemed to love the great wooly beasts.
I got a lump in my throat each time the pick-axe
was slid into the hump of the not-yet-dead.
Then, on page thirty-eight, in the margins, a scribble:
Bring little Samuel a green hide as a memento.

4.

I put the book down and begged of it and clutched.
I walked thirty-three feet into the moon
that somehow bled back broken plates of sorrow.
Yes, it was the full moon over Livermore, bathing
the Laramie Plains. But it was also the killing
moon over Dodge. The abalone moon over Abilene.

5.

Still writing the possum, I corrected
the untanned salutation to say, Dear *Opossum*.
Then I finished dressing the rest of the letter,
before it lost its winter rode, *I am living in the Ohouse of*
    the Ogreen
Buffalo Hides. Nothing is Ogreen here in this Ohouse.
It is just a little washout Oroofed-in with Ogreen-green hides.

6.

How might a word my mouth?
How might what's missing most miss?
How, why, and in what way are we to belief, believe, begin?
For how long and for whom do we remain untreated?
Yes, it was the full moon over Livermore, bathing my brain,
but also the blistering moon over Big Timber. Over mine
    tailings in Butte.

7.

When the wolfer arrived with his strychnine
and traps, the Breaks of the Missouri
seemed to widen, as if the earth itself was tearing apart.
Buttes. Draws. The buffalo hunter responded by bringing:
    one cook
stove with pipe; three wall tents; one saddle horse and three
    wagons;
three sheets of patch paper; and thirty Wilson skinning
    knives.

8.

Dear watery wing of the owl.
Graze my save and my knoll.
Grant me the safe of nightly speak.
Possum my mouth with *this* penance and *that*.
Blink thy sacred eye, like a human—upper lid
down—not like other birds that mark the world in reverse.

9.

A kneeling position with armrests

was preferred by those who prayed.

Make the kill in as small an area as possible,

they whispered to no one in particular, burrowing into
the incision

point in the heart. Eliminate all darkness. Journey there
only

at night, like any nocturnal beast, in search of voles, mice,
mites.

A THEORY OF TAXIDERMY

after an evening in the saloon of The Grand Hotel,
founded in 1890, Big Timber, Montana

Water was so deep we ate bread.
The bar was full of dead animals
with proud contented gaze. The bullet
or the bow brought peace? Not on your life,
but on theirs, as Montana trains exchanged
couplings out back for coal. Winter was hard.
Chickens scratched the grass, pecked their own eggs
open as if trying to grasp the essence
of their own ass. That's the way it is sometimes.
You stare at a map of Chicago
and pray that the tape on the wall won't stick.
French paint is the last thing you need
when scouring your lower intestine
with a candle. It would be easier
to imagine feeding a sparrow gin
and directing its beak with your left hand
in slow ovals over your desk.
Where is the window, and how might you bleed?
How might you carve an egg of light
as a way out? How might a simple apple
of glass become a bullet hole
intended for public display, for allayed

squawks and alleged snorts above the booth?
Geese frozen in flight. Bighorn Sheep sizing
both you and your conspicuous coffee up.
That enormous Elk on the juke box wall
old as the only lodge in town that took its name.
The Santa Fe is surely not transporting hay
to Butte. Winter grass was hard as chicken scratch
on gold plaques, trophy printing far too easy to read.
Everywhere dead animals on the heavenly wall
had the look of knowing what stood
behind brown vacant glass. Eyes shot inward
like a Monet lily swallowing a bridge,
like frightened eggs at the spring pleading.

AMNESIA OF THE HARDBOILED DETECTIVE NOVEL

for James Crumley, 1939-2008

*Crumley was long gone when I got there. Only the alcohol
fumes remained, and the stories.* I knew John must be
right. I could smell kerosene on my red flannel plaid.
Later that afternoon, the redhead strolled into my
office with a pair of legs. I was not her elder and she
was not my dream. Honestly, if it hadn't been for the
autopsy, I would never have looked in the mirror. I
kept searching for lost parts of myself I'd implanted,
through thousands of fantasies, into the bodies of
women I barely knew. I much preferred Celtic sea salt
to sprinkling my food with sea lice. They'd leave a trail
of too much desire for the oceanic carvings of the flesh.
Crumley's characters answer the wrong milk of life.
I kept trying to write myself out of my past. Sure, I
adored breasts. Yes, my parents' divorce bit my wrist.
So that afternoon when the redhead wore that tight
white top and crossed her mysterious hose, I gravitated
toward the gray of her blazer. It was neither black nor
white. It was not something to be solved. Nothing
would be the death of me. I knew danger when I saw
my face in the mirror. In those days everything was a
window. I was like one of those starlings battling myself
in the freshly watered glass. *I was long gone when I got to
the world. Only their perfume from former lives remained,*

and the glory. I knew John must be right. That's the way
it is with karma. We drag our past back through the
future we hope to make alert. I knew I must be wrong. I
could count on it as surely as I could bleed. I could smell
owl resin on my wrist. I'd flown too many missions
across the cloud-embittered moon. Sliced this life away
and that. I'd searched for mice in all the wrong hovels. I
was convinced that crushed bone might make me wrong
if I ate the nervous twitch. So I went to the other office
where the clients came with crime. I carried a .38 that
was really a book and wore a hat. I started not to drink,
thought better of it, and returned to cranberries and
cane syrup. Some sweetness in life had been missing
fifty-six years. Some poem. I'd too long left it in the
bush, with the burning bees and entrails of musk ox. I'd
too long left it in the gorgeous forest between her thighs.
Crumley's characters were Montana-hard. Often on the
lam on the Yellowstone River or North Boulder. I kept
allying myself with Indiana and Colorado. I believed the
border of everything offered the possibility of retreat.
So much more of me kept sinking into the left side of
everything. So many times my left hand wrote with my
right. Like when I took to lying on the sidewalk crack to
seek balance, measure whether my back was in perfect
sway. Yes, I adored her breasts. So for seventeen minutes
that afternoon, I was not her father and she was not
my horse. *Crumley was long gone when I got there? No,
Crumley was long wrong when I arrived. Only desire*

remained, and the horny. John told me so when he spoke
of fumes. Of the kerosene rag stuffed in my chest. Of
the hole that had once been my heart. Smoke lingering
off the cigarette of Bogie or Bacall. The grainy reach of
my black and white 114-minute past. *I'd say Crumley is
the heir apparent to Raymond Chandler.* The review was
true. How all things resolve, though originally confuse.
How the actors remain beautiful youth. How we wake
from the big sleep of our past into who we do.

LETTER TO FORREST FROM LARAMIE

You have the handsomest name, Forrest, east
of the Mississippi. Whole land tracts bow to you.
Fireflies fierce upon your tree. If you were here,
I'd call you Medicine Bow Mike. I'm sure
I'd see snowcaps increasing years in your hair,
as you'd ease down from the high-country
beaver pools for a week of whiskey and cards.
They've certainly camped in mine, refusing to leave.
Such squatters throwing snow seem to like me
more each year. In Laramie, I'm passing
through, up for the day from Colorado,
pretending I'm not already passing fast this life.
We lunched at Coal Creek, an outdoor café
that likes Bootsie, and she, the scent of cowboys
and cream. There was a Great Pyrenees named George.
He was a benevolent king. I never felt so small with him
ponying over our little hound. I thought of your deliberate
and slow. The way you make the world seem seen.
Large. Across the street, Night Heron Books is not
a woodlands goose but a hole claiming Laramie sane.
It says there's feed, and not just a bag of oats
as a horse's sling. In the store. On the shelf.
You were there, your *Deeds of Utmost
Kindness*. Which is all you say and do. *Hey Mike*,
I'd whisper if you were standing with me, leaning
into your buckskin rough. *Read me one of them fallen*

sounds alone in a forest only philosophers can hear.
Gentle me, gentle man, over the timber beaver
can't wait to sink. And you'd roll your sleeve,
drop your calm animal cap, and let your blood
right there into a cup and say that was your poem.
Then slit your best wrist all the way, saving the other
for straws. I could draw the shortest
vein and win the night watch, high on the rise,
overlooking the trains. They couple, out back,
off South First, near Big Hollow Food Co-op.
Who, such days, would name a grocery *hollow?*
Who would claim such emptiness large?
How often our want. How deep and wide
and sky. How we crawl and scrawl
and mound of emptiness, a badger
den of depth. That's where I reside, you know.
In the midnight fierce, pounding out
from the coyotes. With Lorca's ants
that can't be seen but frequent
your wrist. Mary Ann has enough sense
to draw me up from the well-depths
of dirt on the Rawhide Flats, point me
back to the marsh, which seems to be this Night Heron
Books where I find you utmost forever kind, though shelved
in the F's as if your last name was wide and dark
and reach. Imagine a bird balancing a leg, unseen
by clay, sinking into the blathering
musk of a night scent so deep we have to sing.

LETTER TO MICHELLE FROM VICTOR

Scrabblings of dusk. Conjugated grief. Some dead,
dying, died. Workers working still the mines. Michelle,
we might secondsay the heat, admit July, Colorado-
dry, into our bones. Profess to know the many sways.
Feldspar and gold. We might bow before the ciborium
of sunset cutting back across this lack or that, high here
in Victor. 9,695 feet. The Colorado Labor Wars. Union
strikes still struck. Like a lantern about to tip. Deaths
still dead. Sea-gone groan. The strange mouthings of
primitive fish high in rock and tight. The way religion
promulgates the past. There was a little girl in a long
denim skirt went door to door for Christ. Her father,
a pastor. Her mother saw the end of the world, all the
way from Bedford, Indiana to Oskaloosa. Iowa is more
than farming animals and calm. Sometimes our past
unscrews our shoes. You step this way, that. Have taken
strides away from Bible-Belt life. One buckle. Two. How
were you and I born into the same breath? Why this
incarnation here, now?

Mary Ann says Victor is more than ghosts. The Ashanti
Mining Company stoking Rocky Mountain gold all
the way back to Johannesburg, lugging it out of the
bones of the many-soaked. Miners coughing dust as if
two packs of Luckies a day. Backwards, the lines try to
survive. Slavs in Pueblo. Ludlow Greeks. The German
dead of Victor. Dead, dying, decried. Masked. As if.

As if morality was not a play. Right and wrong never
performed. As if Euripides was not an Athenian. *He saw
the veins of men as a net the gods made to catch us in like
wild beasts*, the poet wrote. And was right. Here, now.
Just five miles southeast of Cripple Creek, this town
can't walk. Five miles from where it gave the gold and
built a name. Gave all its blood and hurt. This place of
graves. M.M. Demeree. Ella Porter. Minnie Denson.
Two dogs named Shep. Donkey dust of mules gone
quick over the sluicey ledge. The horse part of the mule
all panic-ear and twitch. We have been made by truly
two, multiples of moaning dust. We have been children
far too long. You still walk door to door inside your
most private. Test this latch and that. Lug the donkey
dust of your father's church into how and why you
cry. I, too, flinch at the voice of strain. Parents who no
longer loved, even themselves. Who in feeling unloved
just tried to survive. Strange mouthings of almost-
human pain. Dry and tight in the shy animal spine.
This raccoon or that. Fox blood in our sleep. Possum
our mouths out with toads. Mary Ann calls it quaint.
The old Victor Hotel. This ghost-town most. A town of
445. Only a brothel-turned-breakfast joint. One rail of
men who exhaust the mine, hunched at the bar called
The Young Buck. And all those boarded doors. News-
papered glass. Ranch-hand sad. 10,000 feet, you'd think,
would be closer to the Lord of Hosts. Like a lantern
that in losing its grip tips heaven light to hay.

We are all burning up inside for mine-dusting the light.
Your father was a church. Does well, you say, with grief.
My mother and father and I divorced at age three. One-
one thousand, two. Children's games are voice. Count
the seconds about to be our lives. Why this life for us
this life now? You and I destined to meet? Victor doesn't
stand for Victory but for the man who tossed his name
into a hat. We should all be so lucky to be christened by
chance. Backwards, we turn to our past for shoes. Step
inside. This foot, that. Walk with our maculate hands.
Drag our monkey-knuckled self to the mineral shelf.
The Western Federation of Miners is dead as a thrown-
bolt latch. Strike, struck, strucked. Conjugate the match.
Friction the boot. Drag the sulfur up through the sole
of the foot into our most fretful stance. Secondsay the
heat. We are here, Michelle—ingots of ignoble birth,
brilliants of light then dead. The strange mouthings of
fish. Mimes caught in the pant. Fossilized and fixed.
The sea-gone groan. Found in this town. Found only in
rock in the search for gold. Dynamite-blast and pick-axe
stance. The strange strained wraithings of now.

THE ANTELOPE TREE

It killed you to see it—not the tree
but the antelope leg dangling
from it, part star, part scar,
cached, perhaps, by a big cat
from the hills. A deer not fifty yards
from it, grazing off Sheep Mountain
Road. Wood ticks must be grumbling
her flesh. The live animal,
or the dead one? You are neither
alive nor dead, you think,
the almost-full moon firing
the pines, one day from whole, one chunk
either side of complete. Something eating
its light, or feeding it.

COLORADO SHEEP WARS, 1894

> "Thirty-eight hundred sheep were stampeded [by
> angry cattlemen] over a bluff into Parachute Creek on
> September 10th while their owners were at the Peach
> Day celebration in Grand Junction.... A posse from
> Parachute found a mass of dead sheep at the foot of a
> thousand-foot bluff..."
>
> —*Craig Courier*, September 14, 1894

The how and why they died. The pleading eye. The I
can't forget. They couldn't talk. Walk. True north in
Colorado is how they ate the lush of it and died. The
Bear River Valley and all that sad. The how and why
I cry. All southern Wyoming wide. Something keeps
mashing, keeps smashing me with cloven hooves and
wool. No, jumping off a cliff is not cliché. Stampeding,
less so. Anything we do is dread weight. Wait here, I'd
say. And I'd get down on all fours and swim the river
sog into my fleece. No, they couldn't walk. Ticks clung
to their swim. Stones to under their hoof. Hooves. We
must cross. We must cross our mouths out with stones.
Cobble together our fierce. The distance between *here*
and *here* is always *there*. Show me your arm's length, and
I'll demonstrate beautiful human demise. Of all the
animals of Parachute Creek, they are dead and most
dying. Alive. Like words. The Union Pacific coupling

cars on the track. Laramie and back. Stampeding the
mouth's scar. Brandish the Circle K. Say it's for *Craig*
or *Courier* or the *cursive cut of something wrong*. Carve
my heart out with soap. The wash the wool the rain
across the plains. Tell me the newsprint is strong. That
unlike the herd, it can talk. Hear. That the café. That
Cheyenne. That the hostess with the bad tattoo will
shiver me a bowl of stew, finger me one night with sweet
regret. We are marked with many scars. She with me,
I with her desire for my desire to save the world with
a word. The hungry of it and quick. Her shoulder that
carries the sad. I might finger her sweat with regret. We
might our mouths. We might kiss and finger and secret
the ink. Not coals cut hot in wooly flesh or grass. Not
the horizontal pupil in the eye. The bah bah bawling
of before and beautiful. No, never the wide of the eye.
Forgive us their death, I'd say, directly into her thigh.
How to jump off a cliff and survive. The erotic size of all
things said. Sad. Of the secret war of how the grass was
won. Of death driving death off a bluff forever into the
pounding mouth of now.

THE WATER TRADE

THE WATER TRADE

Those were the days I subsisted solely on the Water
Trade. Memories of a previous birth night after night
between the thighs of strangers in Tokyo's Shimbashi
district.

*

I have a confession. I have something to say. Please.
Listen. I did not visit Cassie in Buffalo, Wyoming on
July 18th. Nor on the 25th and 27th. I need to tell you.
There was not a storm. I did not discern eels in my
spine. I want you to know lightning did not jump off
the Big Horns into me. Did not light upon her face in
strange moth movements making the kerosene. Did not
stutter-shove my liquid moan back up into my complete
and almost.

If they tell you different, hear me, it is not so. Please.
I want you. I did not want seventeen minutes in stiff
parlor red with two fingers of whiskey. Did not tremble
into her room when they called my name. Did not let
her wash my penis in the bowl beforehand. Never let
her touch me how and where it hurt. Come. Hear me.
I did not _____ into her _____. Nor did I remove the
_____ afterwards like a burning _____. Could not
would not and touch. Please, I have a storm to make.

Here, in my chest. Give me time and I will ignite.
Buffalo, Wyoming is a sad, lonely sound in the middle
of the word-town of my mouth.

*

A bordello in Denver is not a Japanese whorehouse.

*

The Water Trade is a fluid birth. Nights of dancing.
Koto music. Thirteen strings. Luck. A joke walks into
a bar and orders *sake*. Another joke sidles up to it and
says, *Hey big boy, buy me a* _____. Geisha give me
wise, give me warmth. Give me myself moist and make
the wide of your thigh. There are many superstitions we
cannot laugh. Many such lucks among the prostitutes of
Japan. I have heard them before in just-after pillow talk.
A half an hour rest for just 2,000 yen more.

*

George Kalamaras, I hate you—tenderly and with hope.
Perhaps I hate most your Vallejo, his most, your word-
blur and spur. Word seeking word seeking dirt. The
constant urge or tug of tongue toward this thigh and
that.

*

There was a boy grew up with a hole in his art. Each portrait he painted contained negative space. Each tongue he tugged cried from behind. Poems poured out onto the sheet like empty space. Thick, private. Sea-sound salt. Sparrow secretions from his ear. A boy. There was a hole who was a boy. (Private note to John: let me hide, let me retreat things into my hermit self, say it again, see *my most moist*, see *the owl on fire fiercely in my chest.*)

*

What, then, *is* a literary *tour de force*? How might a poem my mouth? How could she? How could her breasts have so much and so dearly throughout my entire and my thigh, marking moist my mouth? A boy of just eight and his unsuspecting aunt? Infinite swirl in the number's curl. Inguinal urge in the soak of her blouse bobbing before me in the lake.

Let me say it again, this time for the world to tear, to rip apart like rain: I could have died right there to have forever and her arms.

*

The Water Trade reflects excess.

The Water Trade is dirt.

The Water Trade could be seen in the stillest of eyes. In pools of the heart when it is much at rest.

In it could be reflected the slopes of demoiselle cranes flying low over the Chungnan Mountains.

In it can be seen what can rarely bleed.

In it can be heard what is never urged.

Through it can be touched what is much mouthed in the dark.

The Water Trade is like a best friend who, in dying, has never died.

*

Okay. Not just Buffalo, Wyoming, but Denver. Pueblo. Lulu City.

Pueblo Prostitutes in 1885

Josie Austin, age 16, birthplace: New York
Annie Bower, 26, birthplace: Louisiana
Edith Burns, 21, Indiana
Rosa DeSoto, 35, Mexico

Mae Dudley, 27, Massachusetts
Lulu Flynn, 28, Virginia
Cora Hicks, 20, Massachusetts
B. Holmes, 17, Missouri
Attie Lee, 22, Indiana
Alice McConnant, 21, Indiana (I am not making this up!)
Sydney Noble, 40, Connecticut
Maud River, 20, Texas (of course she's named *river*)
Isabel Robinson, only 16, Missouri
Allison Ruby, 21, Indiana (what is it about Indiana?)
Alice Sayer, 19, Ohio
Belle Sherwood, 25, Ohio
Jennie Smith, 26, Indiana (okay, no comment)
Madge Thomas, 26, Colorado
Ida Warren, 17, Wales
Louisa Williams, 20, Minnesota

*

If they tell you anything remotely erotic, it is not so.
Please. Listen. Wanted, wanting, want. The sad of her sad
life. The *Okay-I've-got-a-roof*. The *no-place-left-to-go*. Do
stallions really have twenty-six-inch penises when erect
and ejaculate within six to nine seconds of entry? What
is premature? Fifty-three seconds of me inside her or
turning away from the mirror at dawn? I did not could
not tremble or touch. Did not let her wash my hair in the
fishbowl afterwards. Never let her touch me how and why
I clutch. Please, I have a mouth to make. Whole. Here, on

my tongue. Worlds appear, dissolve, in the saliva pools
of speech. Give me time to ignite. The owl. The owl on
fire fiercely in the boy's chest. It is unfair the way the
woman bobbed there in the lake before me at age eight,
before I knew the words for *love* or *hope* or *Tammany
Hall*, the *Bagnio*, or the *Bucket of Blood*, all in Pueblo's
100 block of South Avenue.

*

And so, the high quiet meadows of the Medicine Bow.

And so, Livermore, Colorado, where one *lives* on a
mountain forever *more*.

And so, the way water seeks its own level, the way words
weigh a poem, or longing branches out like beetles
through the pines their insectual branching kills.

*

One learns most about oneself in the saddest and
loneliest dream.

*Ten girls appeared, almost rolling into the room in their
mincing walk. They were fully dressed in ceremonial robes,
and on their faces and necks was the liquid porcelain
powder of their public trade.*

For just 2,000 yen more, there was just-after pillow talk:

> Sitting on steps was bad luck. It drove off customers.
> No small animal—bird, cat, or dog—could cross a
>   room. You had to catch it and send it back to retrace
>   its steps, saying *Go men kudasi* (please excuse me).
> A prayer of good luck by the Auntie of the house at the
>   Good Luck Altar where symbols of the phallus were
>   kept did no harm.
> Sneezing once—someone is saying good things of you.
>   Twice—someone is saying bad things of you. Three
>   times—someone is in love with you. Four times—
>   you've got a cold!
> A basket on your head will make you shorter. Stepping
>   in fresh horse dung will make you grow.
> A child not sensitive to tickling was born a bastard.
> To remove the lint from one's navel will bring on a cold.
> Wax in the ears improves one's memory.
> Curly haired women are lecherous beyond reason.
> A mushroom in the navel cures seasickness.
> Breaking wind turns your tongue yellow for a time.
> Spitting into a privy (*banjo*) will bring on blindness.
> Urinating on an earthworm will cause the penis to swell.
> People with eyebrows too close together don't live long.
> Fan the palms of your hands to cool the whole body.
> Unfilial conduct will give you a hangnail.

*The gestures no longer could be called a dance, or even a game.
It was obscenity: enticing, sexual, yet graceful.*

*

How the West was won. I'm getting hard just writing this.

*

Okay. My greatest fear is not cats or dogs crossing this room or that. Not a hangnail, nor urinating on an earthworm, causing the penis to swell, nor breaking wind and turning the tongue yellow. It is that I will be reborn again and again, begging for more.

*

Okay. Said. Done. Spoken out loud now as if through the body of a sow.

Judy says transform your secret and your most. Make the private sly. Pour the metaphor into a hose attached to the bone glue of the brain.

Patrick says we must live in the poem and die to what creates it.

Don says I need to write a really noisy poem sometime!

Ray says it slantwise, as if it could and might but won't.

Eric doesn't say.

John says, go ahead, piss on the earthworm and feel the
ocean swell.

*

I want, I said. How might I said a poem my mouth?
How could she? How could my aunt's breasts,
unsuspectingly before me in the lake—the damp and
soak of them in her white blouse—have so dearly
throughout my entire and my shy? Years forward and
years bleared back in the muck and mud at my feet. To
be eight years old and forever always wanting more? To
be the number 8. Cruel, curved. Clearly soaked through.
Moistened of my mouth.

*

A bordello in Denver is not a Japanese whorehouse.
If they tell you different, paint out your ears with
soap. Splice your mouth. Allow the sound. Coat the
insides of her privates with Noxzema as a form of
birth control. A bordello in Buffalo is not upstate New
York but a five-street town among antelope and oil
derricks and shots of *Please-let-me-forget-the-ache-of-
being-only-eight*. A bordello in Pueblo is alive with the
drive of many names, even in the Pioneer Cemetery
many of them claim. *Maud, Cora, Isabel. Attie, Alice,
Allison. Belle, Jennie, Madge.* Come. Hear me. Don't
listen to me, stutter-shoved as I am back into a fluid not

quite birthed. Eight. I was only eight. Infinite and sad.
Swirled. Struck since birth. Forever curling into her
bodice, her breasts. In mind alone, if mind could die.
Curling. Back. Into myself. Cleaning, cleansing urge.
The incessant stir of an urgent cur dog.

WORDS HELD BEFORE
IN THE MOUTHS OF THE DEAD

THE MINING CAMPS OF THE MOUTH

He spoke with words that had been held before in the
mouths of the dead. Words like *wistful* and *wildfire*.
In the mining camps of the Medicine Bow all healing
hurts. *Once, when I was young, I was dead*, said the
man about to be my life. The mouth moistens hard as
glands gone sad. At least in Hygiene in high-country
summer. Where the consumptive come to coax the
air. All going comes to Colorado. All coming leaves
desire decried. There is no paradox up high when one
stinks of the inner depths. *Despair is overrated*, I heard
slantwise through the throat of the many-soaked. *Why
it rhymes with "repair" is one of the Seven Wonders of the
World*. One of my many pasts had finally caught up
with me. Reed-bound, mummified. It spoke, she spoke,
he smoked in a barrel of water his last severe brand.
Against the leaning shed, where calves moaned *no*, they
stacked the hot iron, sizzling with names. Not names
but pictographs. Not graphs but hieroglyphs from
deep within the ranch: *The Oxbow; The Circle Shade;
The West-of-Dodge*. Honestly, I read one word at a time,
one line of burnt hide. Note : instructions for how to
be alive : draw each brand, with precision, before your
cowboy license is revoked. Note : instructions for how
to be dead : *be* dead. What burns into us our saddle-
tramp name is new leather creaking old. Ore bags slung
over the rump of a mule. Poor things are sterile, you

know. Like any offspring of a donkey and a cottonwood.
Get yourself a horse. Lead it to water. Make it stink. *You*
try sitting unshaven for twenty-three days on the cattle
drive from Abilene to Dodge and see if your creaking
groin is leather or gold. I spoke with words that had
been held before in her sexual folds. Words like *pink*
and *moist*. Words like *swollen* and *obsessed*. In the mining
camps of my mouth, I kept bending over a pan of her
purest gold. Leaping up into me like wildfire. Even at
high altitude columbine grow. The lung is an amazing
organ. An origami crane in the chest. We need new
names just to breathe. Names of destruction and love.
Names that wing us into the ever-hopeful West. Names
that send our unexamined stool samples to Hygiene. To
correct our tubercular tense—past, present, and nerves.
Names that are ranch-hand sad. There are, of course,
Seven Wonders of both the Ancient and Modern
Worlds. There's the Temple of Artemis at Ephesus, of
course. Chronicled by Callimachus of Cyrene. Which
sounds remarkably like Kalamaras of Serene. The
serenity, of course, of burying a burro on the high-
country pass. Something tender and dear and sad is
always carrying us up and over ourselves, into the time
of no crime and many soothing sheep. Not names, but
hands. Not hands, but a new kind of ranch: *The I've-
Been-a-Jerk; The Oh-I'm-Sorry; The Will-I-Ever-Find?*
Honestly, I bled one word at a time. Note : instructions
for how to love : it spoke, she spoke, *he* spoke. Note :

instructions for how to be alive : *be* alive, coax the folds of your tongue, the words that had been before in the mouths of the dead.

KATYA WHITCOMB

March 12, 1867, aged 3 Ys 8 Ms 12 Ds

At least they gave you a most beautiful place.
If I had loved even your finger, I would have grieved.
Somehow, I do. Here, on the old Buckeye
in what was once the town of Boxelder, your parents
farmed hard. All I know seems sudden,
shocked in your sod. We honor your death
as we might grieve thanks to the moon for a grand
companion. I said the creek is your magnificent
mixed-blood way. I always wanted an Indian mother
called Kate. A father who didn't give in
to the hardship of dirt. No one is playing
in your yard. Eldon Ackerman ranches it
now, tells me within the first hour of friendship
that he and his wife will also be buried
on this rise. He loves a perfect stranger.
He's taken the end of the day
to guide us to your grave, surrounded still
by rail your father split, splinters
decaying right down into your
space. I'm sure you were beautiful, little one.
You barely wore gingham. I could likely count
in my palm butterfly time you caught
in three brief years. You are flying away.
You have been here since 1867.

You are a hummingbird hovering near
my wife's red hair, probing for snowmelt
from the mountains drawing closer, moving
sunset into us. Prickly pears at your feet keep away
the snakes. Eldon says he killed thirty
rattlers just last year. Your parents had
160 acres of homestead, proved it up
with a structure within twelve months.
Your solitary grave is all that's left
of the original ranch. Even the rumor
of two strays at your side are someone's dream
of Indians and their unmarked
hard. Life in the prairie winds
breaks your breath back across the Rawhide Flats.
You are floating and you are ribbed
deep in the earth, even in my cough
as I gentle your dust back to the car
and drive it all the way to Cheyenne.
Didn't you once say, *I love you?*
Wasn't I not there to answer, *Me too?*
If I had loved even a finger or toe, dear one,
I would have shamed the town into your name.
Boxelder is gone. The Buckeye Ranch too.
Your bones remain, dusting the crust of cattle
caught in the graze, giving us what little meat
we might be lucky enough to eat
before we sink into the sinking
sound of grass browning now.

ELEGY FOR JOHN CIPOLLINA: ELECTRIC GUITAR GUNSLINGER

> *"Memory is weak on some details, but I keenly recall sharing a joint with Cipollina, who was dying at the time from emphysema, and watching him strap on his guitar, light up a Lucky Strike and reach for his walker to head to the stage, cigarette hanging from his lip, guitar slung over his shoulder. It was an act of pure defiance, spitting in the face of nothing less than death itself, a rock and roll gunfighter walking out for one more shoot-out, heedless of his pending doom."*

—Joel Selvin

There are many ways to be a cowboy, John. You weren't always sad, picking your axe, slanting sunset-hope into us. The prose poem is made of sentences. The body of the paragraph. Our body, one long sentence. I said *um* seventeen times in a single minute. I counted. The video doesn't lie. That DVD of you in Germany piercing a Lucky onto a tuning key at the end of your guitar. Something is always crucifying something else as it crucifies itself. Iconography can't itch the scratch of worlds in reverse. *Um* could be *Mu* if transposed, the Zen equivalent of the Supreme Now. But you are not now, at least in the body, though you stir again in the paragraph's ash. In the stirrups of the inner ear. We

must consider revising verb confusions as we ride our
words backwards into our lives. Saddlebags on the
Appaloosa on the cover of Quicksilver's *Happy Trails*
could be flapping the road back. But back to where?
What? There is filler in our lives. *Ums* and *uhs* in place
of *OM*. Sometimes it's a cigarette. Sometimes, a joint.
Perhaps we touch ourselves in the intimate dark. Not
just the addicted are addicted to addiction. I breed
sea lice in the salt flats of my words. Take a sentence
and rub it up against the perspiration of my wife's left
breast. There are many ways to be a gunslinger, John.
Sometimes it's John Wayne just to lean on a walker
on the Red River Trail across the stage. Whitman
echoed Wordsworth who echoed badger-scratch in
the Abilene dust. Sometimes our filler fills a hole
with hurt. Dirt dusting the burning leaves leaves our
music sore. Saddle-tramped and blistered. Or was that
you plucking the string, drawing vibrato from your
whammy bar as if water from a bell, as if cowpokes had
camped in your hair all life long? There are ways. There
are many. There are too many ways to have our hurt.
The time of emphysema and the time to defy. *Anyone
who makes plans for after the revolution is a reactionary*,
Bakunin said. *Today is a good day to shy*, answered Red
Cloud at the Treaty of Fort Laramie. The prose poem
is made of sentences. Scratch. Itch. Tuck. Your music,
one long chord you somehow pulled out of thin hair,
Lucky Strike dangling from your lip. The burnt leaves of

your leave-taking stuck-struck gold in the mine shafts
of your lung. Lean on it, John. Roll your own. This
time of cowboys and musk. Of guitar messengers and
messenger services. Of silver quickening the sad-glad
of your heart. You didn't always limp, dragging a spur
like that through the high-noon dust. *Um*, I say. *Um,
um, um*. Between words. Between worlds. Against the
desperation of your desperado plea. Even from your
grave, outlaw man, you still plant your axe in our ear,
slanting sunset-hope right through us.

HISTORY OF A DROWNED DOOR

Red Feather Lakes, Colorado

We're left to imagine too much : fear, struggle, the last
breath. And all that depth. We're left with nothing but
names carved into a post office door, displayed now
in a museum. Simple wood, likely pine, from the high
country. Lodge pole. Ponderosa. Seasons no longer turn,
dead inside the door since they were broken at the root.
I'm no carpenter, but I'd say 80 or 81 x 30. Numbers
don't help. Only matter as a way to plane the space
we cannot possibly fathom. To keep one room from
another. To separate a life. There's almost not enough
room on the door for the names of all who've drowned
in Red Feather Lakes. Names I'm sure I've heard before
either in simple conversation, or from remnants of
a picnic scum-stuck in mountain-lake mud. Nettie
Worley. Rudolf Romero. Ella Torgny. A door drowning
in the names of the drowned. Names spoken years later,
sometimes hushed : a mother's bedtime murmur, sister
remembering a little brother as her best friend tries
to apply makeup, sobs in the Chapel in the Pines off
Red Feather Lakes Road from a man who swears from
this day forward and until death he won't have another
drink. Death is never whispered water. Only drunk. In
names preserved on a door. In the promise of the waves.
Held, as it is, in the long cords of the throat. It seeps out

into all sorts of talk, from the merits of stamp collecting
to *We need a new bulb above the kitchen sink* to *Darling,
did you remember to take out the trash?* Strange how
slantwise our word, how sorry the throat. How light
when it cannot possibly get in. Words mosquito-borne
as *Morocco* and *Namibia* and *French Equatorial Africa*
sound remarkably like *Be sure to separate the bottles and
the cans.* There is no explanation, never enough frame on
which to hang such a door. We walk through too many
spaces, saying words private and less private, public and
touch, moving from here to there with the makings of
our mouths, only rarely shaking door-thunder loose
from finger-soak. And all we absorb. The final breaths
of fish as they frantic themselves onto shore as if there
was now not enough room. On the door. In the lake. In
the tentative nerves leading back to the cold calling of
their brain. Wherever I turn in this museum, there is a
closed window begging for boards. Names claiming the
kingdom of mud and sorrow. People and dread. Bertha.
Verda. Clarence and Cecile. Even that lost horse and
burro from the Darrow Ranch on the ridge. All the
uncarved dead in all the unnamed places of lakes rarely
fed. Spring-fed, from beneath. We're left to imagine far
too much. Split. Infinite. To fear of it and struggle and
breath. Yes, *breath* not *breathe.* Names now in a door are
no longer nouns but verbs. Word-sunk that has spent
decades in fish-scale and muck rises into our lives : to
run : to eat : to breathe.

THIRD ELEGY

for Barney, for Gene

Start with a word fractured in threes
    as a way into not knowing how, why, or in what way
    gender bends the signature thread of blood
          Mary Ann   Barney   me
      I've said it required not knowing
and I meant every shed of my speech, Gene, as if it depended on
          my life of language
      warm within the confines of concentric cuts
    under the tongue   as if all the frozen fish
    of the world suddenly thawed
in the saliva pools of sleep   birthing a bag of cold-blooded
         brethren   Warmed,
    we see its possibilities, taste it in the oatmeal moments
      of morning light   even its blight
        and the chlorosis of insufficient green
    The French toast suddenly there   at the Renaissance in
                 Fort Wayne
        in Albuquerque at Mannie's
         like a possible language lean
        into the sweet resistance of cinnamon savoring
               the tongue
Yes, it's the cinnamon that takes the way we speak
    tastes us toward something sweet   like a god of ancient
               Israel calling forth

the fire that has already swept

                                    up
                        a son's hair
            The owl on fire fiercely in the boy's chest
                                may be a commitment
        toward relinquishing our will to the great wagging
                    of this tongue or that
                            to mouthing the minute passings
                                the multiple bloodlettings
                of what we may never understand
                may be a way to say we love   we truly love
                            any lullified leeching   or
                            the burning bird more than birth
Meditation, like a fluid rib, also burns
                        though fears away the dross
            tells me a strong blue light   persistent
        surrounds this house with love   with your love
        eighty-three years and counting
                        And the dog's   the dog who left
        the body July 11 at 2:06 p.m.   who left my body my
                                        Abraham
                            my pile of dry brush
                                and saving grave
                    The dog you also loved and whose name
                                        I need
                    not speak   but do
    in the wake of each day
                        in the bend the hairs

of my arm   the translation of sad
        The sad sad glance of it all
        in membering her Friday   each Friday
                the number II in the cut
                        of every letter of every
                earth
in the tearing out of my hair
        And the tongue of all mouths
through which I speak you speak, as well, Gene,
        as if you weren't alive or dead
                or continuously leaving
                the eaves   your driveway on
                                Mesa Verde NE
                and what you left on either side
        in those two
                cypress trees
                Because you loved her too, told me
                so
                        as you kissed me goodbye
                        kissed my lip
        as I held her to say so long to you
                that last   time
You touched her hair,
                petted her black beagle body, her
                                sweet beagle ear
                held it in your hand the last you said the time
                saying, *Barney's a good girl   such a good
                dog*   That name

the gift the gender bend the signature
of love
the halo hunt of my secret glorious hound self
through which my breathing
bends and   blurs   and breathes   still
and always
will
and begs to
be
a word started   a word broken but begun
into three

THE GRAVE WITCHERS

"*The radio that told me about the death of Billy The Kid*"

—Jack Spicer

The radio that told me my bones. The radio stirring the home of the dead up into them. Those rods made of steel, coat hangers, plastic, glass. Marrow like never-nouns of milk. The ground beset with babies. Watchfires on the rise. Slutgrass, deer mice, and sleep. Guns traded for whiskey. Whiskey soaped for touch. The false guns of a life well-deathed.

*

Take a rod. Dowse it down a line of sight. Keep the thumb out of the way, the hands low enough not to interfere with the rod's reach. Read the poem for the *sake* of the poem. Read the poem, read the poem, read the poem. The slow syllable crunch of the tongue. Like the breaking soft of bones. Snap the flap of skin tied to the mouth. Take a rod. The two rods will realign of their own accord from parallel oceans to crossed-over-the-grave.

*

What often happens is life gets in the way. Of life itself.
Of death. Of the liminal in-between. What often
happens is books ask to be alive. What often comes is
linen in the skin. Muslin in the mouth. I can no more
recall whether the random rain is a meaningless shadow
or the grave itself. Crawling down, in rich animal rinse,
from the Medicine Bow. Sure, Michelle was bit in Tie
Siding that afternoon by fire ants at the grave of Tunis
Blodgett or Patrick McHugh. Yes, I unlatched the
cemetery's barbed wire gate, begging the cut go calm. Of
course, Mary Ann brought her flower-bouquet self unto
and across each unmarked scar. What often happens
often comes. Rain raining rain raining rain. A word
breaking like thistleberry over the strained soft burial of
the tongue.

*

Here is where the Utes killed fifty-three Cherokees
that winter. There is where their voice. The rods don't
lie, stirring now toward the underneath of trailers,
cabins, cattle brands, stacks. The chorus of domesticated
barking back to coyote-howl in the star-sunk night.
Cherokee Park is home to more than little rain and
Colorado July biting the bones.

*

Tips Still Needed to Find Burials:

1. Frank Winnons, who drowned at Poudre Falls
   in June 1884 when he was 27. Reports say:
   "Body found 2 miles below falls. Frank Kelley,
   Ed Gearhart, and (Mr.) Stewart made a coffin of
   cottonwood and buried him near the river."

2. Charles Hall, who drowned in the Poudre near
   Rustic. The June 18, 1884, and June 25, 1884, issues
   of *The Evening Courier* report a coffin was sent up
   by mule-team to the site.

3. Frank Kelley, who drowned in the Poudre July
   18, 1885. (The same Frank Kelley as per number
   1 above.) Reports say his body was found "near
   George Grill's place 2 miles above Home P.O.
   Buried there 10/10/1886."

4. Molly McBride, whose long red hair drowned
   below my tongue, December 3, 1966, in the saliva
   pools of sleep. A coffin was carried into fourth
   grade math, hidden along the inside flap of the
   book, *The Secret Workings of Algebra and You*.

5. Debbie Crouch, whose loose blouse and no bra the
   following year in Mr. Stuart's class at MacArthur
   Elementary (not the same Mr. Stewart as per

number 1 above), exposed a full minute her
budding left breast, buried—in an undisclosed
location—somewhere north of my groin, south of
the throat.

6. My cousin, George Avgerinos, MIA in Vietnam,
   March 6, 1969. Found one month later. Casket
   closed. Aunt June could not bear to see her son.
   Only Uncle Ted and my father identified the
   remains. Buried in South Holland, Illinois, at
   what passed as his funeral, but lost in the foliage
   of my thirteen-year-old tongue, tied in iron combs.

7. A 1959 Greek divorce divorced before the boy
   could say *Upanishad*, or *Vallejo*, or *The owl on fire
   fierce in my chest*.

Anyone with information on these or other remote
burials may call Donna or Doug Knowles at 555-0111.

*

A radio stirring the groan. A radio that told the death.
Rods made of plastic. Glass. The ground beset with
dried begonias of the blood. With grave regret. Sweat
bees in the buried brains. Slutgrass in our sheared
sleep. Bah bah in the bygone breeze. In the pine tree's
sap. Saddest, they say, is discovering a child laid to rest
outside the family plot. Pick a rod. Any rod. Dowse the

ground. Turn it toward the blight. The dead are dead, dying, died. Conjugated borders. Bursts. Bees. Like searching slow for tired water. Bradded in the catches. In the assonant. In the slatch. Birthed, of course, at breach. Bonestrewn buttes. Tick fever in the cattle-stance. Footlamps sunk into the Judas Hole several poems deep.

*

Don't ask me how it works, said Doug Knowles, a retired chemist and ceramicist who has been dowsing for graves in Larimer County for four years. *I just know a line of poetry when it leaps up and lodges between my toes, vibrating there like acres of aching space.*

*

Was the late Evan Roberts in Livermore, they say, who'd heard it from his father, George, that baby graves, like very old graves, have a weaker reading on the rods. Like rain in the Medicine Bow never crawling down to the plains. Like an unfinished poem, glimpsed slantwise through a left breast, tugging years the tough of the tongue. All the way into being a man. Like an almost loved. A maybe. A what if. Separate from the slake and slutch of such and such. What could have possibly been.

DREAM IN WHICH FRANK WATERS IS MY MOTHER

It wasn't the bolo tie, though it did connect its umbilical
cord self to that mountain core of turquoise at his
throat. Nor was it the way he made the morning
muffins, greeting me when I woke and descended the
stair as if the word *oatmeal* might save the world. *Burnt
toast*, I'd told him, rubbing my eye. *In bed, near my toes.*
And he sent me back up to care for the crusts. When I
returned, Frank was sewing a patch on my jeans. *This is
how my own mother did it when I was born many moons
west in Colorado Springs*, he told me. *Here, hold this slip
of thread between your lips, and try to keep it in place
while mouthing the word "camel."* Dark parts of my scar
were apparently flaking off. Frank acted as if I wasn't
becoming a man, as if the moist dents in the sheet he'd
change weekly were nothing but the water of stars when
they came to die. I sat and tried to smoke a rose, Frank
telling me the thorns would stunt my growth. That
I should be careful to clean up any curve of crust my
starlit body might cut. *It's natural*, he said. *Nothing for
shame. Remember*, he continued, *it's easier for an antelope
to pass through the eye of a crow than for a living man to
be dead.* Somehow, he made sense. Frank Waters sense.
As if my mother and divorced father were tiny rivulets
I no longer needed to ignore. From my core, a turquoise
bolo suddenly around my *own* neck. Calming my throat.
The stone, he said, *Cerrillos turquoise. It's such a shame.*

Now all the Cerrillos is mined out. Like the gold and silver near Pikes Peak where I was born to my own pair of dark stars. I smelled oranges and saw Frank pasting the glaze over a muffin. He'd put down the needle and thread and was carefully making a swirl. This way, that. As if both ends of its sugary comet tail might collide at muffin's edge, like a snake circling back to eat itself whole. *This is the way of the Hopi,* he continued. *The ones who dance the snakes and never get bit. Remember, it's easier to grieve than to mouth the sound of now.* Then he sent me back up to care for the crusts. *Careful,* he said, *and be tender with yourself.* My body giving off dark drops of watery stars like globs of cold oats as I took the stair.

I'M WRITING GENE A LETTER

in memory of the poet Gene Frumkin

I'm writing Gene a letter but he's dead.
I keep trying to say it's 99
in Fort Collins today but only 93
in Albuquerque. I keep trying his side
with my hand, the resurrection of his word.
Remember the Indian who sold us cedar?
I had a headache three days and could kill it
only in Livermore after dumping
the bundle from my backseat.

Remember the fragrance of the full moon
over Dodge? I'm writing Bob my mouth,
the tender of it and clutch. The way this word
or that. The moist imprint of my strain.
Trains don't always reach West, I'd say,
and he'd nod that rain-in-the-barrel nod
he'd use as table water in Vermont, Susan
each evening at the stitch, dirty shirt
left out on the truck to wash and dry.

I can't write Alvaro because I love him.
No one can write another they see
as themselves. No one agrees. Nothing.
Not even the pronouns. So I'm writing

Alvaro through Gene because Bob
just published his book. Alvaro's book,
not Gene's. Made by Bob's hand.
My book in a way. And Tom McGrath's,
because he kept writing Gene
a note. I keep writing

John because he's not dead, because he writes me
back each day as if I'm answering myself,
as if he's unleashed the fire ants
of Namibia again in my wrist.
In a way I'm writing Bob, though sometimes I call
him Patrick. I begin, *Dear Rain-in-My-Chest*,
or *Dear Zhivago platting the full Yuriatan moon
over Dodge*, or *Sad, Sad Glance of the Owl*.
I call Patrick a name. My name. Paul's.
Barney. Bootsie. Adorable-Beagle-Breath.
Because Gene loved them both,
though he died before Bootsie arrived.

I can't write Gene because he's alive.
Somewhere busy. Marking my strain.
He keeps saying, *Hey, amigo, don't write me
anymore. I'm fried. Write Bob*, though they never met.
I think Gene wants to write Alvaro
so is asking me to write Bob.
I think John wants to live in DeKalb
forever, even if it's not the West,

maybe because I'm writing him
how much I need to stay alive.
I think how Patrick and Paul loved Barney
and will love her even more
through Bootsie when they meet.
Bob loves them all in his rain-in-the-barrel
way, and through Kokomo, his cat,
who keeps napping as if Gene hasn't died.
As if Bob has left Vermont
and is capturing the full moon
over Dodge from a train that keeps trying
the loping rails west.

So I'll visit Alvaro in New Mexico
and not write. A letter, that is,
though I'll still skill the sky.
Because I love him, as I love Gene,
even though Gene's tired of me
disturbing his rest. Though it's eternal,
so one more letter can't mean much.
Maybe I'll write Eric
before seeing Alvaro because Gene loved Eric
too. Even before Gene died.
As he loved my wrist. The one red
with ants swollen in bitten blood.
The blood John sends back to me each day
when he writes to help me somehow stay alive.

A PREFACE TO THE WEST

PREFACE TO THE SECOND EDITION OF THE WEST

The preponderance of the West gathered here was composed by my shoes. The West, like poetry, is most often walking away.[1]

Ever since the West—the *real* West—died, it has been suggested that a posthumous edition of this fascinating location and state of mind be compiled, replete with all the West's subsequent turbulence, treaties, sometimes-peace, and consumptive coughing. This edition, therefore, has been a monumental undertaking, the composition of this preface equally so, for a poet who dares to write location—and not just *about* location—can only be measured by his spurs, a spur's life work often imprinting upon a culture only after transmigration of a myth sinks into the soft flanks of the most noble horse poetry it bites into as it tries to ride off.

Sunset. Forgiveness. Hope for a new word. Or, at the very least, a language capable of forgiving a sunset its always-step-ahead, out-of-reach bruise before rider and mount.

This is an introduction to the reader's sagacity, a West *about* the making of the West.

---

1 Indeed, this is a preface to the composition of the *actual* West, not a book, much less a book of poems about it. Furthermore, it is *not* an afterword, except only in the sense that the travails of the West—the *real* West—have been known to neutralize all sorts of opposites: before and after; yesterday and a day; blood and less blood; and before-blood and death.

Like location, it has been suggested that certain poets
would not in fact exist without invisibility. Take, for
example, the blurred, blue ink writing the name *George
Kalamaras* backwards so that it can only be read in a
mirror.[2] It would do us well to recall that Geronimo had
no mirrors. Nor Bret Harte. Nor Billy the Kid. Nor any
of the nine players of the Miko Kings—that almost-
forgotten 1907 baseball team of Native Americans in
Ada, queen city of Indian Territory (later comprising
the state of Oklahoma).

Jack London, on the contrary, had seven or eight
mirrors, depending, of course, on the number of dogs,
and on how he and Klondike Mike Mahoney harnessed
them to deliver the mail.

I am saying that if Vallejo did not exist, the West—the
real West—would have been forced to manifest his
destiny as an unspoken chest, feed him to the sheep,
which would in turn be fed to the wolves, and to place
his poems in a leather pouch that would subsequently
be delivered to, to make love with, Kalamaras's mother
(through a process of psychic osmosis) when she was
twenty-three and wanting and shy. Thus sent, his
Peruvian seed would have blown all the way to Chicago,
by way of December and ponies and rail.

---

2 See *Secrets of the Backwards Handwriting of Leonardo da Vinci*,
pages 33, 44, 55, 66, 77, and 88.

I am certain the reader can understand the urgency of
such words. Thus, a second collection[3] will no doubt
need to be compiled at a later date, dropped down the
depths of a Yellowstone geyser at rest, and periodically
shot back out like sea lice through a sperm whale's
blowhole, as if clearing a congested prostate.

Do not be construed, dear reader. Do not come un-
shoed. In short, walk away from these words.

The present volume builds, then, upon all of the West's
previous pain, including malice, starvation, and trickery,
even the seemingly trivial publications not offered by the
literary elite, including but not limited to cowboy chaps
impersonating a chapbook, or the scratching of psoriac
pamphlets, or the long-out-of-print deaths, some of
which never made it into the news, much less the depths
of cavernous knowing. We have therefore labored to
include all the missing deaths herewith, correcting
any obvious typographical errors in the way a person
died. It has come to our attention, for example, that
sometimes at the final moment the breath eased out
through the anus, or that fierce crows flung themselves
through bullet holes in the chest of the unshot. There
are mule teams of the unexplained, lugging the intellect
through the great salt flats on a cat's tongue. While
earlier editions approached the West only as a metaphor of
Manifold Density, we have labored to include fugitive love-

---

3 Not to be confused with a sperm collection.

makings between strangers, but only those west of Dodge, yet as far south as the Abilene and Chisholm Trails.

In other words, when I mention Debbie Crouch and Cindy Funk (and her mysterious hose), please be advised that I loved them both as much as a ten-year-old possibly could and subconsciously wanted to fuck each before I even knew what fucking was. I place before you Exhibit A—otherwise known as *Fourth and Fifth Grades*. On the wall, a map of Colorado. Above it, the entire sky, Wyoming-wide. Geography was an option to die. Choose any point and fix your gaze upon it while growing up so as to shut out the rest of the whirl. One could stare at the east wall where, ironically, a map of the West held sway, and sense the place below the skin where all opposites burn, resolving eventually toward dissolve. The swish swish of Cindy walking past my desk, placing her sheet of misspelled words in the teacher's tray. Then that very same swish swooshing through the sound of every word I ever thought I held, dissolved suddenly in the aching nouns of now. Consider, as well, Exhibit B—otherwise known as *Furtive Rides West of Dodge and as Far South as My Arm Allowed*. How is it that the Chisholm Trail always leads back up and into one's own scrotum?

In other words, I grew up in Indiana watching tireless episodes of *Rawhide* and *Wagon Train*, of *Bonanza*,

Gunsmoke, and *Have Gun Will Travel*. In other words,
I grew up in Indiana watching myself die. Sometimes
I was the hero. Other times, the hero's hero. On rare
Saturday nights, I'd take a break from gunfire and tough
talk and watch wrestlers like Buddy Rogers, an hour
before the bullfights were broadcast live from Mexico
City. I never wanted to be the matador or the bull or
the silly clown, only the crack in the lance as it fell out
of the wounded spine and gave the bull back its breath,
so it could charge the stands. *I'm just resting my eyes*, the
boy would say, late at night when his family encouraged
him to bed. But it wasn't a boy or even me, only the
West—the *real* West—resting its bet on a straight flush,
Queen of Hearts high.

Thus, this edition is meant to correct the early sexual
yearnings of both the poet *and* the West, when they
both fell helplessly in love with Debbie or Cindy or Miss
Kitty. With the Queen's breasts felt somehow through
the card's laminate and expressed in a derringer-shot
across green felt, or in the dog's tender licking as it
curled into itself trying to clean away the day's dust. The
lives collected here should not be read as a "collection"
in the narrowest sense. Any attempt to gather the
West forces, by the very nature of the attempt, turkey
buzzards back into the decaying sap oozing from the
cottonwood's crack. One could imagine other orderings
of the West, an anthology from the perspective of

Japan,[4] for example, that explored Chinese saloons and the bones of Mongolian ponies crushed for dice and thrown out onto the bars, or a collection of various kinds of wind in the belly of a cow, both before slaughter and moments after.

What we mean is that the West—the *real* West—is neither dead nor alive. In this case, Steve McQueen in *Wanted: Dead or Alive* may have wandered into a dust storm where *either* and *or*, *death* and *life*, did not exist— a paradigm shift where the wrong dry goods store on the wrong street in a wrong Colorado town composed of Wyoming dust only sold buttons for bullets for his sawed-off rifle that he kept as a holstered gun.

This current edition seeks to correct the West by placing it east of itself. And then placing it again east of that, all the way around, until like some primordial beast it coils back to swallow its own tail, and in the swallowing ingests a side of itself it could never have blessed. In short, sometimes the most sacred taboo is profane, and eating ourselves is our most instructive food.

We are not at liberty to explain. We have been given limited space,[5] even when a preface appears anywhere but at the onset of our task.

---

4 See, for instance, the published diaries of Akira Kurosawa, Chapter 7, "Rolling the Bones West."

5 Like people given just so many breaths or years in their lives.

We ask, instead, that you examine the cover of the second Quicksilver Messenger Service album, *Happy Trails*.[6] The dust of palominos is embedded in the remarkable spots on the Appaloosa's chest, lodged in the throat of any who listen, read, or well-up at the most desperate of departures. The way each ending yields an ending, every beginning, a burning. Sunrise moving blood-let into us.

The rider on the album jacket is flapping his hat goodbye. To the woman. To her petticoat. To fourth and fifth grade lust. To a lifetime of longing thereof. To the way station on the plains that saved. The West gathered there and here is gathered in dust. A supplement of ghosts is available upon written request.

---

6 Moaning is acceptable when listening to the track, "Mona." Loving oneself is discouraged when listening to "Who Do You Love?"

NOTES

The book's epigraph and the epigraph for "The Grave Witchers" are drawn from *The Collected Books of Jack Spicer*, Black Sparrow Press, 1975.

"House of Green Buffalo Hides. Slabs of Hump at Right, January 1882": The epigraph is from *The Frontier Years*, by Mark H. Brown and W. R. Felton, Bramhall House, 1955. The phrases in section one, "A sitting position with rest sticks / was preferred by most" and *"Make the kill / in as small an area as possible,"* and the list of supplies in section seven, are adapted from this source. The actual name of the photo the poem is based on is, "House of Green Buffalo Hides. Slabs of Hump at Right, North Montana, January 1882."

"Letter to Michelle from Victor": The phrase, *"He saw the veins of men as a net the gods made to catch us in like wild beasts,"* is from "Euripides the Athenian," by George Seferis, *Collected Poems*, Princeton University Press, 1981. Translated by Edmund Keeley and Philip Sherrard.

"The Water Trade": The phrase, "George Kalamaras, I hate you—tenderly and with hope," is an adaptation of the line, "César Vallejo, I hate you with tenderness!" César Vallejo, *The Complete Posthumous Poetry*,

translated by Clayton Eshleman and José Rubia
Barcia, University of California Press, 1978. The list of
superstitions of Japanese prostitutes is adapted from
the book, *Yoshiwara: City of the Senses*, by Stephen
and Ethel Longstreet, David McKay Company,
Inc., 1970. The italicized paragraphs in that section
immediately before and after the superstitions are
taken verbatim from the same text. The list of names
of Pueblo prostitutes (though not the parenthetical
commentary) is taken from *Brothels, Bordellos, & Bad
Girls: Prostitution in Colorado, 1860-1930*, by Jan MacKell,
University of New Mexico Press, 2004.

"Katya Whitcomb" is dedicated to Eldon Ackerman.

"Elegy for John Cipollina: Electric Guitar Gunslinger":
The epigraph is from an article by Joel Selvin, from his
internet column, *Smart Ass: The Music Journalism of Joel
Selvin*, December 10, 2010. This poem is dedicated to
Ray Gonzalez, my brother in all things Cipollina.

"The Grave Witchers": The first three of seven "Tips
Still Needed to Find Burials" are taken from an article
on grave witchers by Linda Bell, "Dowsing Methods
Used to Find County Graves," *North Forty News*
(Livermore, Colorado), February 2004. I have also
quoted and adapted material from the article for the
section beginning, *"Don't ask me how it works…"* This
poem is dedicated to Linda Bell for her assistance in
first telling me about the grave witchers.

ACKNOWLEDGMENTS

The author thanks the editors of the following magazines in which some of these poems, or their previous versions, first appeared:

The Bitter Oleander: "Dream in Which Frank Waters Is
    My Mother"
The Bloomsbury Review: "Elegy for John Cipollina:
    Electric Guitar Gunslinger"
Boulevard: "A Theory of Taxidermy"
Calibanonline: "Me. Mine. Moist. Exposed in the
    Medicine Bow"
Columbia Poetry Review: "The Death of Nikola Tesla,"
    "Amnesia of the Hardboiled Detective Novel," and
    "Third Elegy"
Copper Nickel: "Colorado Sheep Wars, 1894" (finalist for
    the 2012 *Copper Nickel* Contest in Poetry)
Cutthroat, A Journal of the Arts: "House of Green
    Buffalo Hides. Slabs of Hump at Right, January 1882"
    (finalist for the 2011 Joy Harjo Poetry Award)
Denver Quarterly: "The Mining Camps of the Mouth"
Hunger Mountain: "The Antelope Tree"
Malpaís Review: "I'm Writing Gene a Letter"

Gratitude to Jefferson Hansen and *AlteredScale.com*
for featuring an audio reading by the author of "Third
Elegy."

Thanks, as well, to the Indiana Arts Commission for an Individual Artist's Fellowship (2011) and Indiana University-Purdue University Fort Wayne for a 2011 summer faculty research grant, both of which contributed to the writing of this book.

The author thanks his wife, Mary Ann Cain, for her unending love, inspiration, and support. He also offers gratitude for the friendship and great assistance of John Bradley, for his invaluable commentary on this book and for being the first to read most of these poems. He thanks Bob ("Del Gato") Arnold for all his sun-soaked insights and moon-lathed words across the Laramie Plains. The author is deeply grateful for the support of his family, especially his mother, Georgina Allen, and many friends, in particular those who offered insight and conversation regarding this project: Eric Baus, Michelle Comstock, Ray Gonzalez, Patrick Lawler, Paul B. Roth, Bill Tremblay, Sue Tungate, and John Zimmerman. Heartfelt thanks, as well, to Ander Monson for selecting this book as winner of the New Michigan Press/*DIAGRAM* Chapbook Contest and for his design and editing skills in seeing it into publication.

COLOPHON

Text is set in a digital version of Jenson, designed by Robert Slimbach in 1996, and based on the work of punchcutter, printer, and publisher Nicolas Jenson. The titles are in Futura.

☙ ☞

GEORGE KALAMARAS is Professor of English at Indiana University-Purdue University Fort Wayne, where he has taught since 1990. He is the author of six books of poetry and seven poetry chapbooks, including *Kingdom of Throat-Stuck Luck* (2012), winner of the Elixir Press Poetry Prize. After living many years with their beagle, Barney, George and his wife, writer Mary Ann Cain, have welcomed a new beagle pup, Bootsie, into their home. They live in Fort Wayne, Indiana, and regularly return to northern Colorado, where George and Mary Ann lived for several years in the 1980s.

NEW MICHIGAN PRESS, based in Tucson, Arizona, prints poetry and prose chapbooks, especially work that transcends traditional genre. Together with DIAGRAM, NMP sponsors a yearly chapbook competition.

DIAGRAM, a journal of text, art, and schematic, is published bimonthly at THEDIAGRAM.COM. Periodic print anthologies are available from the New Michigan Press at NEWMICHIGANPRESS.COM/NMP.